This Journal Belongs To:

_____

"Have patience with all things - but first with yourself. Never confuse your mistakes with your value as a human being. You are a perfectly valuable, creative, and worthwhile person simply because you exist. And no amount of triumphs or tribulations can ever change that."

-Saint Francis de Sales

Each daily journal page consists of writing down what you are thankful for, duh! But just as important you are prompted to express WHY you are thankful. There are 90 of these daily pages.

At the bottom there is a place to jot down people to pray for. This can also include souls in Purgatory.

There are four "prompt" pages throughout to help with reflection.

A Note from the Authors

We created this journal specifically for Catholic women.

With all of the daily struggles that come with raising a family, it is easy to forget the blessings we have in our lives. The stresses of work, educating the kids, sickness, financial issues, miscarriages, family conflict, car problems, death, depression, anxiety, pandemics, etc. can blind us.

Or you may have a vocation in the religious life, or are a single lay person, which comes with its own set of challenges.

If you are reading this you probably have: a place to live, food, transportation, and family/friends that care about you.

Those things are important but they are only temporal. Most of all let us be thankful for our love of God.

Thank God for the small things you encounter each day.

God Bless You!

My Catholic Planners and Journals is operated by a Catholic couple with 7 kids. We have "normal" lives and jobs. We are hoping to continue building this business and to provide more Catholic related books.

We would really appreciate it if you please leave us a review. Each review is personally read by us and it helps us to know the needs and wants of our customers.
Go here to do so:

https://www.amazon.com/author/mycatholicplanners

Date:_____

Thanks Be to God for:

_____
_____
_____
_____
_____

Why I am Thankful:

_____
_____
_____
_____
_____

Good Things that Happened Today:

_____
_____
_____
_____
_____

People to Pray For:

_____
_____
_____
_____

I will praise you, LORD, with all my heart;
I will declare all your wondrous deeds. – Psalm 9:2

Date:_____

Thanks Be to God for:

_____

_____

_____

_____

_____

_____

Why I am Thankful:

_____

_____

_____

_____

_____

Good Things that Happened Today:

_____

_____

_____

_____

_____

People to Pray For:

_____

_____

_____

_____

I will praise you, LORD, with all my heart;
I will declare all your wondrous deeds. – Psalm 9:2

Date: _____

Thanks Be to God for:

_____
_____
_____
_____
_____

Why I am Thankful:

_____
_____
_____
_____

Good Things that Happened Today:

_____
_____
_____
_____

People to Pray For:

_____
_____
_____
_____

I will praise you, LORD, with all my heart;
I will declare all your wondrous deeds. – Psalm 9:2

Date: _____

Thanks Be to God for:

_____
_____
_____
_____
_____
_____

Why I am Thankful:

_____
_____
_____
_____
_____

Good Things that Happened Today:

_____
_____
_____
_____
_____

People to Pray For:

_____
_____
_____
_____
_____

I will praise you, LORD, with all my heart;
I will declare all your wondrous deeds. – Psalm 9:2

Thanks Be to God for:

_____

_____

_____

_____

_____

Why I am Thankful:

_____

_____

_____

_____

Good Things that Happened Today:

_____

_____

_____

_____

People to Pray For:

_____

_____

_____

_____

I will praise you, LORD, with all my heart;
I will declare all your wondrous deeds. – Psalm 9:2

Date:_____

Thanks Be to God for:

_____
_____
_____
_____
_____
_____

Why I am Thankful:

_____
_____
_____
_____
_____
_____

Good Things that Happened Today:

_____
_____
_____
_____
_____

People to Pray For:

_____
_____
_____
_____

I will praise you, LORD, with all my heart;
I will declare all your wondrous deeds. – Psalm 9:2

Date: _____

Thanks Be to God for:

_____

_____

_____

_____

_____

Why I am Thankful:

_____

_____

_____

_____

Good Things that Happened Today:

_____

_____

_____

_____

People to Pray For:

_____

_____

_____

_____

I will praise you, LORD, with all my heart;
I will declare all your wondrous deeds. – Psalm 9:2

Date:_____

Thanks Be to God for:

_____
_____
_____
_____
_____
_____

Why I am Thankful:

_____
_____
_____
_____
_____

Good Things that Happened Today:

_____
_____
_____
_____
_____

People to Pray For:

_____
_____
_____
_____
_____

I will praise you, LORD, with all my heart;
I will declare all your wondrous deeds. – Psalm 9:2

Date: _____

Thanks Be to God for:

_____
_____
_____
_____
_____

Why I am Thankful:

_____
_____
_____
_____

Good Things that Happened Today:

_____
_____
_____
_____

People to Pray For:

_____
_____
_____
_____

I will praise you, LORD, with all my heart;
I will declare all your wondrous deeds. – Psalm 9:2

Date:_____

Thanks Be to God for:

_____
_____
_____
_____
_____
_____

Why I am Thankful:

_____
_____
_____
_____
_____

Good Things that Happened Today:

_____
_____
_____
_____
_____

People to Pray For:

_____
_____
_____
_____
_____

I will praise you, LORD, with all my heart;
I will declare all your wondrous deeds. – Psalm 9:2

Date:_____

Thanks Be to God for:

_____
_____
_____
_____
_____

Why I am Thankful:

_____
_____
_____
_____

Good Things that Happened Today:

_____
_____
_____
_____

People to Pray For:

_____
_____
_____
_____

I will praise you, LORD, with all my heart;
I will declare all your wondrous deeds. – Psalm 9:2

Date:_____

Thanks Be to God for:

_____
_____
_____
_____
_____
_____

Why I am Thankful:

_____
_____
_____
_____
_____
_____

Good Things that Happened Today:

_____
_____
_____
_____
_____

People to Pray For:

_____
_____
_____
_____
_____

I will praise you, LORD, with all my heart;
I will declare all your wondrous deeds. – Psalm 9:2

Date:_____

Thanks Be to God for:

_____
_____
_____
_____
_____

Why I am Thankful:

_____
_____
_____
_____
_____

Good Things that Happened Today:

_____
_____
_____
_____
_____

People to Pray For:

_____
_____
_____
_____

I will praise you, LORD, with all my heart;
I will declare all your wondrous deeds. – Psalm 9:2

Date:_____

Thanks Be to God for:

_____
_____
_____
_____
_____
_____

Why I am Thankful:

_____
_____
_____
_____
_____

Good Things that Happened Today:

_____
_____
_____
_____
_____

People to Pray For:

_____
_____
_____
_____
_____

I will praise you, LORD, with all my heart;
I will declare all your wondrous deeds. – Psalm 9:2

Thanks Be to God for:

_____
_____
_____
_____
_____

Why I am Thankful:

_____
_____
_____
_____

Good Things that Happened Today:

_____
_____
_____
_____

People to Pray For:

_____
_____
_____
_____

I will praise you, LORD, with all my heart;
I will declare all your wondrous deeds. – Psalm 9:2

Date:_____

Thanks Be to God for:
_____
_____
_____
_____
_____

Why I am Thankful:
_____
_____
_____
_____
_____

Good Things that Happened Today:
_____
_____
_____
_____
_____

People to Pray For:
_____
_____
_____
_____

I will praise you, LORD, with all my heart;
I will declare all your wondrous deeds. – Psalm 9:2

Date:_____

Thanks Be to God for:

_____

_____

_____

_____

_____

Why I am Thankful:

_____

_____

_____

_____

_____

Good Things that Happened Today:

_____

_____

_____

_____

_____

People to Pray For:

_____

_____

_____

_____

_____

I will praise you, LORD, with all my heart;
I will declare all your wondrous deeds. – Psalm 9:2

Date:_____

Thanks Be to God for:

_____

_____

_____

_____

_____

Why I am Thankful:

_____

_____

_____

_____

_____

Good Things that Happened Today:

_____

_____

_____

_____

_____

People to Pray For:

_____

_____

_____

_____

I will praise you, LORD, with all my heart;
I will declare all your wondrous deeds. – Psalm 9:2

Date:_____

Thanks Be to God for:

_____

_____

_____

_____

_____

Why I am Thankful:

_____

_____

_____

_____

Good Things that Happened Today:

_____

_____

_____

_____

People to Pray For:

_____

_____

_____

_____

I will praise you, LORD, with all my heart;
I will declare all your wondrous deeds. – Psalm 9:2

Date: _____

Thanks Be to God for:

_____
_____
_____
_____
_____
_____

Why I am Thankful:

_____
_____
_____
_____
_____

Good Things that Happened Today:

_____
_____
_____
_____
_____

People to Pray For:

_____
_____
_____
_____

I will praise you, LORD, with all my heart;
I will declare all your wondrous deeds. – Psalm 9:2

Date:_____

Thanks Be to God for:

_____
_____
_____
_____
_____

Why I am Thankful:

_____
_____
_____
_____

Good Things that Happened Today:

_____
_____
_____
_____

People to Pray For:

_____
_____
_____
_____

I will praise you, LORD, with all my heart;
I will declare all your wondrous deeds. – Psalm 9:2

Date:_____

Thanks Be to God for:

_____

_____

_____

_____

_____

Why I am Thankful:

_____

_____

_____

_____

_____

Good Things that Happened Today:

_____

_____

_____

_____

_____

People to Pray For:

_____

_____

_____

_____

I will praise you, LORD, with all my heart;
I will declare all your wondrous deeds. – Psalm 9:2

Date: _____

Thanks Be to God for:

_____

_____

_____

_____

_____

Why I am Thankful:

_____

_____

_____

_____

Good Things that Happened Today:

_____

_____

_____

_____

People to Pray For:

_____

_____

_____

_____

I will praise you, LORD, with all my heart;
I will declare all your wondrous deeds. – Psalm 9:2

STOP

Someday it's tough to remember the good things in life. Sometimes our prayer life can seem dry. Here are some questions to ask yourself:

- Do I pray at the start and end of my day?
- Do I examine my conscience at the end of each day?
- How much spiritual reading am I doing?

Jot down a few things you can improve upon each day to help you focus on the good around you.

_____

_____

_____

_____

_____

_____

_____

_____

_____

_____

_____

"Thank God ahead of time."
- Blessed Solanus Casey

Date: _____

Thanks Be to God for:

_____
_____
_____
_____
_____

Why I am Thankful:

_____
_____
_____
_____

Good Things that Happened Today:

_____
_____
_____
_____

People to Pray For:

_____
_____
_____
_____

I will praise you, LORD, with all my heart;
I will declare all your wondrous deeds. – Psalm 9:2

Date:_____

Thanks Be to God for:

_____
_____
_____
_____
_____
_____

Why I am Thankful:

_____
_____
_____
_____
_____

Good Things that Happened Today:

_____
_____
_____
_____
_____

People to Pray For:

_____
_____
_____
_____
_____

I will praise you, LORD, with all my heart;
I will declare all your wondrous deeds. – Psalm 9:2

Date:_____

Thanks Be to God for:

_____
_____
_____
_____
_____

Why I am Thankful:

_____
_____
_____
_____
_____

Good Things that Happened Today:

_____
_____
_____
_____
_____

People to Pray For:

_____
_____
_____
_____
_____

I will praise you, LORD, with all my heart;
I will declare all your wondrous deeds. – Psalm 9:2

Date:_____

Thanks Be to God for:

_____
_____
_____
_____
_____
_____

Why I am Thankful:

_____
_____
_____
_____
_____

Good Things that Happened Today:

_____
_____
_____
_____
_____

People to Pray For:

_____
_____
_____
_____

I will praise you, LORD, with all my heart;
I will declare all your wondrous deeds. – Psalm 9:2

Date: _____

Thanks Be to God for:
_____
_____
_____
_____
_____

Why I am Thankful:
_____
_____
_____
_____
_____

Good Things that Happened Today:
_____
_____
_____
_____
_____

People to Pray For:
_____
_____
_____
_____
_____

I will praise you, LORD, with all my heart;
I will declare all your wondrous deeds. – Psalm 9:2

Date:_____

Thanks Be to God for:

_____
_____
_____
_____
_____

Why I am Thankful:

_____
_____
_____
_____

Good Things that Happened Today:

_____
_____
_____
_____

People to Pray For:

_____
_____
_____
_____

I will praise you, LORD, with all my heart;
I will declare all your wondrous deeds. – Psalm 9:2

Date:_____

Thanks Be to God for:

_____
_____
_____
_____
_____

Why I am Thankful:

_____
_____
_____
_____

Good Things that Happened Today:

_____
_____
_____
_____

People to Pray For:

_____
_____
_____
_____

I will praise you, LORD, with all my heart;
I will declare all your wondrous deeds. – Psalm 9:2

Date: _____

Thanks Be to God for:

_____
_____
_____
_____
_____

Why I am Thankful:

_____
_____
_____
_____

Good Things that Happened Today:

_____
_____
_____
_____

People to Pray For:

_____
_____
_____
_____

I will praise you, LORD, with all my heart;
I will declare all your wondrous deeds. – Psalm 9:2

Date: _____

Thanks Be to God for:

_____
_____
_____
_____
_____

Why I am Thankful:

_____
_____
_____
_____

Good Things that Happened Today:

_____
_____
_____
_____

People to Pray For:

_____
_____
_____
_____

I will praise you, LORD, with all my heart;
I will declare all your wondrous deeds. – Psalm 9:2

Date:_____

Thanks Be to God for:

_____

_____

_____

_____

_____

Why I am Thankful:

_____

_____

_____

_____

_____

Good Things that Happened Today:

_____

_____

_____

_____

_____

People to Pray For:

_____

_____

_____

_____

I will praise you, LORD, with all my heart;
I will declare all your wondrous deeds. – Psalm 9:2

Date:_____

Thanks Be to God for:

_____
_____
_____
_____
_____

Why I am Thankful:

_____
_____
_____
_____

Good Things that Happened Today:

_____
_____
_____
_____

People to Pray For:

_____
_____
_____
_____

I will praise you, LORD, with all my heart;
I will declare all your wondrous deeds. – Psalm 9:2

Date:_____

Thanks Be to God for:

_____
_____
_____
_____
_____
_____

Why I am Thankful:

_____
_____
_____
_____
_____

Good Things that Happened Today:

_____
_____
_____
_____
_____

People to Pray For:

_____
_____
_____
_____
_____

I will praise you, LORD, with all my heart;
I will declare all your wondrous deeds. – Psalm 9:2

Date:_____

Thanks Be to God for:

_____
_____
_____
_____
_____

Why I am Thankful:

_____
_____
_____
_____

Good Things that Happened Today:

_____
_____
_____
_____

People to Pray For:

_____
_____
_____
_____

I will praise you, LORD, with all my heart;
I will declare all your wondrous deeds. – Psalm 9:2

Date:_____

Thanks Be to God for:

_____
_____
_____
_____
_____
_____

Why I am Thankful:

_____
_____
_____
_____
_____

Good Things that Happened Today:

_____
_____
_____
_____
_____

People to Pray For:

_____
_____
_____
_____

I will praise you, LORD, with all my heart;
I will declare all your wondrous deeds. – Psalm 9:2

Date:_____

Thanks Be to God for:

_____

_____

_____

_____

_____

Why I am Thankful:

_____

_____

_____

_____

Good Things that Happened Today:

_____

_____

_____

_____

People to Pray For:

_____

_____

_____

_____

I will praise you, LORD, with all my heart;
I will declare all your wondrous deeds. – Psalm 9:2

Date:_____

Thanks Be to God for:

_____
_____
_____
_____
_____
_____

Why I am Thankful:

_____
_____
_____
_____
_____

Good Things that Happened Today:

_____
_____
_____
_____
_____

People to Pray For:

_____
_____
_____
_____

I will praise you, LORD, with all my heart;
I will declare all your wondrous deeds. – Psalm 9:2

Date:_____

Thanks Be to God for:

_____

_____

_____

_____

_____

Why I am Thankful:

_____

_____

_____

_____

_____

Good Things that Happened Today:

_____

_____

_____

_____

_____

People to Pray For:

_____

_____

_____

_____

_____

I will praise you, LORD, with all my heart;
I will declare all your wondrous deeds. – Psalm 9:2

Date:_____

Thanks Be to God for:

_____
_____
_____
_____
_____

Why I am Thankful:

_____
_____
_____
_____
_____

Good Things that Happened Today:

_____
_____
_____
_____
_____

People to Pray For:

_____
_____
_____
_____

I will praise you, LORD, with all my heart;
I will declare all your wondrous deeds. – Psalm 9:2

Date:_____

Thanks Be to God for:

_____

_____

_____

_____

_____

Why I am Thankful:

_____

_____

_____

_____

Good Things that Happened Today:

_____

_____

_____

_____

People to Pray For:

_____

_____

_____

_____

I will praise you, LORD, with all my heart;
I will declare all your wondrous deeds. – Psalm 9:2

Date:_____

Thanks Be to God for:

_____
_____
_____
_____
_____
_____

Why I am Thankful:

_____
_____
_____
_____
_____

Good Things that Happened Today:

_____
_____
_____
_____
_____

People to Pray For:

_____
_____
_____
_____

I will praise you, LORD, with all my heart;
I will declare all your wondrous deeds. – Psalm 9:2

Date:_____

Thanks Be to God for:

_____
_____
_____
_____
_____

Why I am Thankful:

_____
_____
_____
_____

Good Things that Happened Today:

_____
_____
_____
_____

People to Pray For:

_____
_____
_____
_____

I will praise you, LORD, with all my heart;
I will declare all your wondrous deeds. – Psalm 9:2

Date:_____

Thanks Be to God for:

_____

_____

_____

_____

_____

Why I am Thankful:

_____

_____

_____

_____

Good Things that Happened Today:

_____

_____

_____

_____

People to Pray For:

_____

_____

_____

_____

I will praise you, LORD, with all my heart;
I will declare all your wondrous deeds. – Psalm 9:2

STOP

As Catholics we know that God allows bad things to happen as He will not interfere with our free will. However, God *can and does* make good come out of evil. Jot down some times where something good came out of what seemed to be a bad situation.

_____

_____

_____

_____

_____

_____

_____

_____

_____

_____

_____

_____

_____

_____

"Thank God ahead of time."
- Blessed Solanus Casey

Date:_____

Thanks Be to God for:

_____

_____

_____

_____

_____

Why I am Thankful:

_____

_____

_____

_____

Good Things that Happened Today:

_____

_____

_____

_____

People to Pray For:

_____

_____

_____

_____

I will praise you, LORD, with all my heart;
I will declare all your wondrous deeds. – Psalm 9:2

Date:_____

Thanks Be to God for:

_____
_____
_____
_____
_____

Why I am Thankful:

_____
_____
_____
_____
_____

Good Things that Happened Today:

_____
_____
_____
_____
_____

People to Pray For:

_____
_____
_____
_____

I will praise you, LORD, with all my heart;
I will declare all your wondrous deeds. – Psalm 9:2

Date:_____

Thanks Be to God for:

_____
_____
_____
_____
_____
_____

Why I am Thankful:

_____
_____
_____
_____
_____

Good Things that Happened Today:

_____
_____
_____
_____
_____

People to Pray For:

_____
_____
_____
_____

I will praise you, LORD, with all my heart;
I will declare all your wondrous deeds. – Psalm 9:2

Thanks Be to God for:

_____

_____

_____

_____

_____

Why I am Thankful:

_____

_____

_____

_____

Good Things that Happened Today:

_____

_____

_____

_____

People to Pray For:

_____

_____

_____

_____

I will praise you, LORD, with all my heart;
I will declare all your wondrous deeds. – Psalm 9:2

Date:_____

Thanks Be to God for:

_____
_____
_____
_____
_____
_____

Why I am Thankful:

_____
_____
_____
_____
_____

Good Things that Happened Today:

_____
_____
_____
_____
_____

People to Pray For:

_____
_____
_____
_____
_____

I will praise you, LORD, with all my heart;
I will declare all your wondrous deeds. – Psalm 9:2

Thanks Be to God for:

_____

_____

_____

_____

_____

Why I am Thankful:

_____

_____

_____

_____

Good Things that Happened Today:

_____

_____

_____

_____

People to Pray For:

_____

_____

_____

_____

I will praise you, LORD, with all my heart;
I will declare all your wondrous deeds. – Psalm 9:2

Date:_____

Thanks Be to God for:

_____
_____
_____
_____
_____
_____

Why I am Thankful:

_____
_____
_____
_____
_____

Good Things that Happened Today:

_____
_____
_____
_____
_____

People to Pray For:

_____
_____
_____
_____
_____

I will praise you, LORD, with all my heart;
I will declare all your wondrous deeds. – Psalm 9:2

Date:_____

Thanks Be to God for:

_____

_____

_____

_____

_____

Why I am Thankful:

_____

_____

_____

_____

Good Things that Happened Today:

_____

_____

_____

_____

People to Pray For:

_____

_____

_____

_____

I will praise you, LORD, with all my heart;
I will declare all your wondrous deeds. – Psalm 9:2

Date: _____

Thanks Be to God for:

_____
_____
_____
_____
_____
_____

Why I am Thankful:

_____
_____
_____
_____
_____

Good Things that Happened Today:

_____
_____
_____
_____
_____

People to Pray For:

_____
_____
_____
_____
_____

I will praise you, LORD, with all my heart;
I will declare all your wondrous deeds. – Psalm 9:2

Thanks Be to God for:

_____

_____

_____

_____

_____

Why I am Thankful:

_____

_____

_____

_____

Good Things that Happened Today:

_____

_____

_____

_____

People to Pray For:

_____

_____

_____

_____

I will praise you, LORD, with all my heart;
I will declare all your wondrous deeds. – Psalm 9:2

Date:_____

Thanks Be to God for:

_____
_____
_____
_____
_____
_____

Why I am Thankful:

_____
_____
_____
_____
_____

Good Things that Happened Today:

_____
_____
_____
_____
_____

People to Pray For:

_____
_____
_____
_____
_____

I will praise you, LORD, with all my heart;
I will declare all your wondrous deeds. – Psalm 9:2

Date:_____

Thanks Be to God for:

_____
_____
_____
_____
_____

Why I am Thankful:

_____
_____
_____
_____

Good Things that Happened Today:

_____
_____
_____
_____

People to Pray For:

_____
_____
_____
_____

I will praise you, LORD, with all my heart;
I will declare all your wondrous deeds. – Psalm 9:2

Date:_____

Thanks Be to God for:

_____
_____
_____
_____
_____

Why I am Thankful:

_____
_____
_____
_____

Good Things that Happened Today:

_____
_____
_____
_____

People to Pray For:

_____
_____
_____
_____

I will praise you, LORD, with all my heart;
I will declare all your wondrous deeds. – Psalm 9:2

*Date:*_____

Thanks Be to God for:

_____

_____

_____

_____

_____

Why I am Thankful:

_____

_____

_____

_____

_____

Good Things that Happened Today:

_____

_____

_____

_____

_____

People to Pray For:

_____

_____

_____

_____

_____

I will praise you, LORD, with all my heart;
I will declare all your wondrous deeds. – Psalm 9:2

Date: _____

Thanks Be to God for:

_____
_____
_____
_____
_____
_____

Why I am Thankful:

_____
_____
_____
_____
_____

Good Things that Happened Today:

_____
_____
_____
_____
_____

People to Pray For:

_____
_____
_____
_____
_____

I will praise you, LORD, with all my heart;
I will declare all your wondrous deeds. – Psalm 9:2

*Date:*_____

Thanks Be to God for:

_____

_____

_____

_____

_____

Why I am Thankful:

_____

_____

_____

_____

Good Things that Happened Today:

_____

_____

_____

_____

People to Pray For:

_____

_____

_____

_____

I will praise you, LORD, with all my heart;
I will declare all your wondrous deeds. – Psalm 9:2

Date:_____

Thanks Be to God for:
_____
_____
_____
_____
_____

Why I am Thankful:
_____
_____
_____
_____

Good Things that Happened Today:
_____
_____
_____
_____
_____

People to Pray For:
_____
_____
_____
_____
_____

I will praise you, LORD, with all my heart;
I will declare all your wondrous deeds. – Psalm 9:2

Date: _____

Thanks Be to God for:

_____
_____
_____
_____

Why I am Thankful:

_____
_____
_____
_____

Good Things that Happened Today:

_____
_____
_____
_____

People to Pray For:

_____
_____
_____
_____

I will praise you, LORD, with all my heart;
I will declare all your wondrous deeds. – Psalm 9:2

Date:_____

Thanks Be to God for:

_____
_____
_____
_____
_____

Why I am Thankful:

_____
_____
_____
_____

Good Things that Happened Today:

_____
_____
_____
_____

People to Pray For:

_____
_____
_____
_____

I will praise you, LORD, with all my heart;
I will declare all your wondrous deeds. – Psalm 9:2

Date:_____

Thanks Be to God for:

_____
_____
_____
_____
_____

Why I am Thankful:

_____
_____
_____
_____

Good Things that Happened Today:

_____
_____
_____
_____

People to Pray For:

_____
_____
_____
_____

I will praise you, LORD, with all my heart;
I will declare all your wondrous deeds. – Psalm 9:2

Date: _____

Thanks Be to God for:

_____
_____
_____
_____
_____
_____

Why I am Thankful:

_____
_____
_____
_____
_____

Good Things that Happened Today:

_____
_____
_____
_____
_____

People to Pray For:

_____
_____
_____
_____

I will praise you, LORD, with all my heart;
I will declare all your wondrous deeds. – Psalm 9:2

Date: _____

Thanks Be to God for:

_____
_____
_____
_____
_____

Why I am Thankful:

_____
_____
_____
_____

Good Things that Happened Today:

_____
_____
_____
_____

People to Pray For:

_____
_____
_____
_____

I will praise you, LORD, with all my heart;
I will declare all your wondrous deeds. – Psalm 9:2

Date:_____

Thanks Be to God for:

_____

_____

_____

_____

_____

_____

Why I am Thankful:

_____

_____

_____

_____

_____

Good Things that Happened Today:

_____

_____

_____

_____

_____

People to Pray For:

_____

_____

_____

_____

I will praise you, LORD, with all my heart;
I will declare all your wondrous deeds. – Psalm 9:2

STOP

God always answers our prayers, however sometimes the answer is "no." Other times God will give us what we are asking for, even if it's not in the exact way we think is best.

Write down some of your recent prayers where God has answered them with some kind of a "yes."

_____

_____

_____

_____

_____

_____

_____

_____

_____

_____

"Thank God ahead of time."
- Blessed Solanus Casey

Date:_____

Thanks Be to God for:

_____
_____
_____
_____
_____
_____

Why I am Thankful:

_____
_____
_____
_____
_____

Good Things that Happened Today:

_____
_____
_____
_____
_____

People to Pray For:

_____
_____
_____
_____
_____

I will praise you, LORD, with all my heart;
I will declare all your wondrous deeds. – Psalm 9:2

Date:_____

Thanks Be to God for:

_____
_____
_____
_____
_____

Why I am Thankful:

_____
_____
_____
_____
_____

Good Things that Happened Today:

_____
_____
_____
_____
_____

People to Pray For:

_____
_____
_____
_____
_____

I will praise you, LORD, with all my heart;
I will declare all your wondrous deeds. – Psalm 9:2

Date:_____

Thanks Be to God for:

_____
_____
_____
_____
_____
_____

Why I am Thankful:

_____
_____
_____
_____
_____

Good Things that Happened Today:

_____
_____
_____
_____
_____

People to Pray For:

_____
_____
_____
_____
_____

I will praise you, LORD, with all my heart;
I will declare all your wondrous deeds. – Psalm 9:2

Date:_____

Thanks Be to God for:

_____
_____
_____
_____
_____

Why I am Thankful:

_____
_____
_____
_____

Good Things that Happened Today:

_____
_____
_____
_____

People to Pray For:

_____
_____
_____
_____

I will praise you, LORD, with all my heart;
I will declare all your wondrous deeds. – Psalm 9:2

Date:_____

Thanks Be to God for:

_____
_____
_____
_____
_____
_____

Why I am Thankful:

_____
_____
_____
_____
_____

Good Things that Happened Today:

_____
_____
_____
_____

People to Pray For:

_____
_____
_____
_____

I will praise you, LORD, with all my heart;
I will declare all your wondrous deeds. – Psalm 9:2

*Date:*_____

Thanks Be to God for:

_____

_____

_____

_____

_____

Why I am Thankful:

_____

_____

_____

_____

Good Things that Happened Today:

_____

_____

_____

_____

People to Pray For:

_____

_____

_____

_____

I will praise you, LORD, with all my heart;
I will declare all your wondrous deeds. – Psalm 9:2

Date:_____

Thanks Be to God for:

_____
_____
_____
_____
_____
_____

Why I am Thankful:

_____
_____
_____
_____
_____

Good Things that Happened Today:

_____
_____
_____
_____
_____

People to Pray For:

_____
_____
_____
_____
_____

I will praise you, LORD, with all my heart;
I will declare all your wondrous deeds. – Psalm 9:2

Date:_____

Thanks Be to God for:

_____
_____
_____
_____
_____

Why I am Thankful:

_____
_____
_____
_____
_____

Good Things that Happened Today:

_____
_____
_____
_____
_____

People to Pray For:

_____
_____
_____
_____
_____

I will praise you, LORD, with all my heart;
I will declare all your wondrous deeds. – Psalm 9:2

Date:_____

Thanks Be to God for:
_____
_____
_____
_____
_____
_____

Why I am Thankful:
_____
_____
_____
_____
_____

Good Things that Happened Today:
_____
_____
_____
_____
_____

People to Pray For:
_____
_____
_____
_____

I will praise you, LORD, with all my heart;
I will declare all your wondrous deeds. – Psalm 9:2

Date:_____

Thanks Be to God for:

_____
_____
_____
_____
_____

Why I am Thankful:

_____
_____
_____
_____

Good Things that Happened Today:

_____
_____
_____
_____

People to Pray For:

_____
_____
_____
_____

I will praise you, LORD, with all my heart;
I will declare all your wondrous deeds. – Psalm 9:2

Date: _____

Thanks Be to God for:

_____
_____
_____
_____
_____

Why I am Thankful:

_____
_____
_____
_____
_____

Good Things that Happened Today:

_____
_____
_____
_____
_____

People to Pray For:

_____
_____
_____
_____
_____

I will praise you, LORD, with all my heart;
I will declare all your wondrous deeds. – Psalm 9:2

Date: _____

Thanks Be to God for:

_____
_____
_____
_____
_____

Why I am Thankful:

_____
_____
_____
_____

Good Things that Happened Today:

_____
_____
_____
_____

People to Pray For:

_____
_____
_____
_____

I will praise you, LORD, with all my heart;
I will declare all your wondrous deeds. – Psalm 9:2

*Date:*_____

Thanks Be to God for:

_____
_____
_____
_____
_____

Why I am Thankful:

_____
_____
_____
_____
_____

Good Things that Happened Today:

_____
_____
_____
_____
_____

People to Pray For:

_____
_____
_____
_____

I will praise you, LORD, with all my heart;
I will declare all your wondrous deeds. – Psalm 9:2

Date:_____

Thanks Be to God for:

_____
_____
_____
_____
_____

Why I am Thankful:

_____
_____
_____
_____

Good Things that Happened Today:

_____
_____
_____
_____

People to Pray For:

_____
_____
_____
_____

I will praise you, LORD, with all my heart;
I will declare all your wondrous deeds. – Psalm 9:2

Date: _____

Thanks Be to God for:

_____
_____
_____
_____
_____
_____

Why I am Thankful:

_____
_____
_____
_____
_____

Good Things that Happened Today:

_____
_____
_____
_____
_____

People to Pray For:

_____
_____
_____
_____
_____

I will praise you, LORD, with all my heart;
I will declare all your wondrous deeds. – Psalm 9:2

Date:_____

Thanks Be to God for:

_____
_____
_____
_____
_____

Why I am Thankful:

_____
_____
_____
_____

Good Things that Happened Today:

_____
_____
_____
_____

People to Pray For:

_____
_____
_____
_____

I will praise you, LORD, with all my heart;
I will declare all your wondrous deeds. – Psalm 9:2

Date:_____

Thanks Be to God for:

_____
_____
_____
_____
_____

Why I am Thankful:

_____
_____
_____
_____

Good Things that Happened Today:

_____
_____
_____
_____

People to Pray For:

_____
_____
_____
_____

I will praise you, LORD, with all my heart;
I will declare all your wondrous deeds. – Psalm 9:2

Date:_____

Thanks Be to God for:

_____
_____
_____
_____
_____

Why I am Thankful:

_____
_____
_____
_____

Good Things that Happened Today:

_____
_____
_____
_____

People to Pray For:

_____
_____
_____
_____
_____

I will praise you, LORD, with all my heart;
I will declare all your wondrous deeds. – Psalm 9:2

Date:_____

Thanks Be to God for:

_____

_____

_____

_____

_____

Why I am Thankful:

_____

_____

_____

_____

_____

Good Things that Happened Today:

_____

_____

_____

_____

_____

People to Pray For:

_____

_____

_____

_____

_____

I will praise you, LORD, with all my heart;
I will declare all your wondrous deeds. – Psalm 9:2

Date:_____

Thanks Be to God for:

_____

_____

_____

_____

_____

Why I am Thankful:

_____

_____

_____

_____

Good Things that Happened Today:

_____

_____

_____

_____

People to Pray For:

_____

_____

_____

_____

I will praise you, LORD, with all my heart;
I will declare all your wondrous deeds. – Psalm 9:2

Date: _____

Thanks Be to God for:

_____
_____
_____
_____
_____
_____

Why I am Thankful:

_____
_____
_____
_____
_____

Good Things that Happened Today:

_____
_____
_____
_____
_____

People to Pray For:

_____
_____
_____
_____

I will praise you, LORD, with all my heart;
I will declare all your wondrous deeds. – Psalm 9:2

Date:_____

Thanks Be to God for:

_____

_____

_____

_____

_____

Why I am Thankful:

_____

_____

_____

_____

Good Things that Happened Today:

_____

_____

_____

_____

People to Pray For:

_____

_____

_____

_____

_____

I will praise you, LORD, with all my heart;
I will declare all your wondrous deeds. – Psalm 9:2

Date: _____

Thanks Be to God for:

_____
_____
_____
_____
_____
_____

Why I am Thankful:

_____
_____
_____
_____
_____

Good Things that Happened Today:

_____
_____
_____
_____
_____

People to Pray For:

_____
_____
_____
_____

I will praise you, LORD, with all my heart;
I will declare all your wondrous deeds. – Psalm 9:2

STOP

Someday it's tough to remember the good things in life. Sometimes our prayer life can seem dry. Here are some questions to ask yourself:

- Am I praying for others or just myself?
- Do I prepare for Mass or am I rushed in getting there?
- Am I praying a rosary everyday either alone or with my family?

Jot down a few things you can improve upon each day to help you focus on the good around you.

_____

_____

_____

_____

_____

_____

_____

_____

_____

_____

"Thank God ahead of time."
- Blessed Solanus Casey

Prayers in Latin

Sign of the Cross:

In nomine Patris, et Filii, et Spiritus Sancti. Amen.

The Lord's Prayer:

PATER NOSTER, qui es in caelis, sanctificetur nomen tuum. Adveniat regnum tuum. Fiat voluntas tua, sicut in caelo et in terra. Panem nostrum quotidianum da nobis hodie, et dimitte nobis debita nostra sicut et nos dimittimus debitoribus nostris. Et ne nos inducas in tentationem, sed libera nos a malo. Amen.

The Hail Mary:

AVE MARIA, gratia plena, Dominus tecum. Benedicta tu in mulieribus, et benedictus fructus ventris tui, Iesus. Sancta Maria, Mater Dei, ora pro nobis peccatoribus, nunc, et in hora mortis nostrae. Amen.

Thank you for purchasing this book.
We hope you found value in this
gratitude journal. Check out our other
journals and planners at
https://www.amazon.com/author/mycat
holicplanners

God Bless!

Made in the USA
Las Vegas, NV
15 August 2023

76134605R00066